AF484644

Life Edited.

Pain. Pleasure. Perspective.

Jameel Haiat

For H,

You have taken my pain and replaced it with love…

With every minute, every hour, every day, we change.
As it has been five years since I originally published *Life Edited*, I too have changed.
My outlook upon life, and quality of life, have changed dramatically since I went through throat cancer diagnosis, treatment and a very lengthy, and still ongoing, recovery.
Words that I use to represent my emotions, my ideas and myself have changed. How I use those words has changed.
So now as I re-release this my first poetry book, I choose to keep my poetry intact, but with some minor iterations that I feel bring some pieces more in-line with the changes of who I am today.
I hope you will still enjoy, are amused and feel inspired from what you find within these pages as much as I do.
Yes, there is change, but sometimes, actually most times, change can be good.

Life.

It can be a real mother fucker.

We all have those days.

Sometimes we step onto the bear trap, crawl through the razor
wire and eat the broken glass.

We carry the weight of the world and drown our emotional self in a
sea of dark, bleak, soul reducing pain and absorb it in our little carbon
hearts.

Then there are the other days.

We wake up with the sweet beautiful smell of puppy breath and
look out across the horizon at those gorgeous, fat, fluffy clouds
filled with light and hope. We can see our dreams, desires and
future out there, somewhere, anywhere, and on that day, we are all
invincible and unstoppable.

It's all about perspective…

Words

Pain.

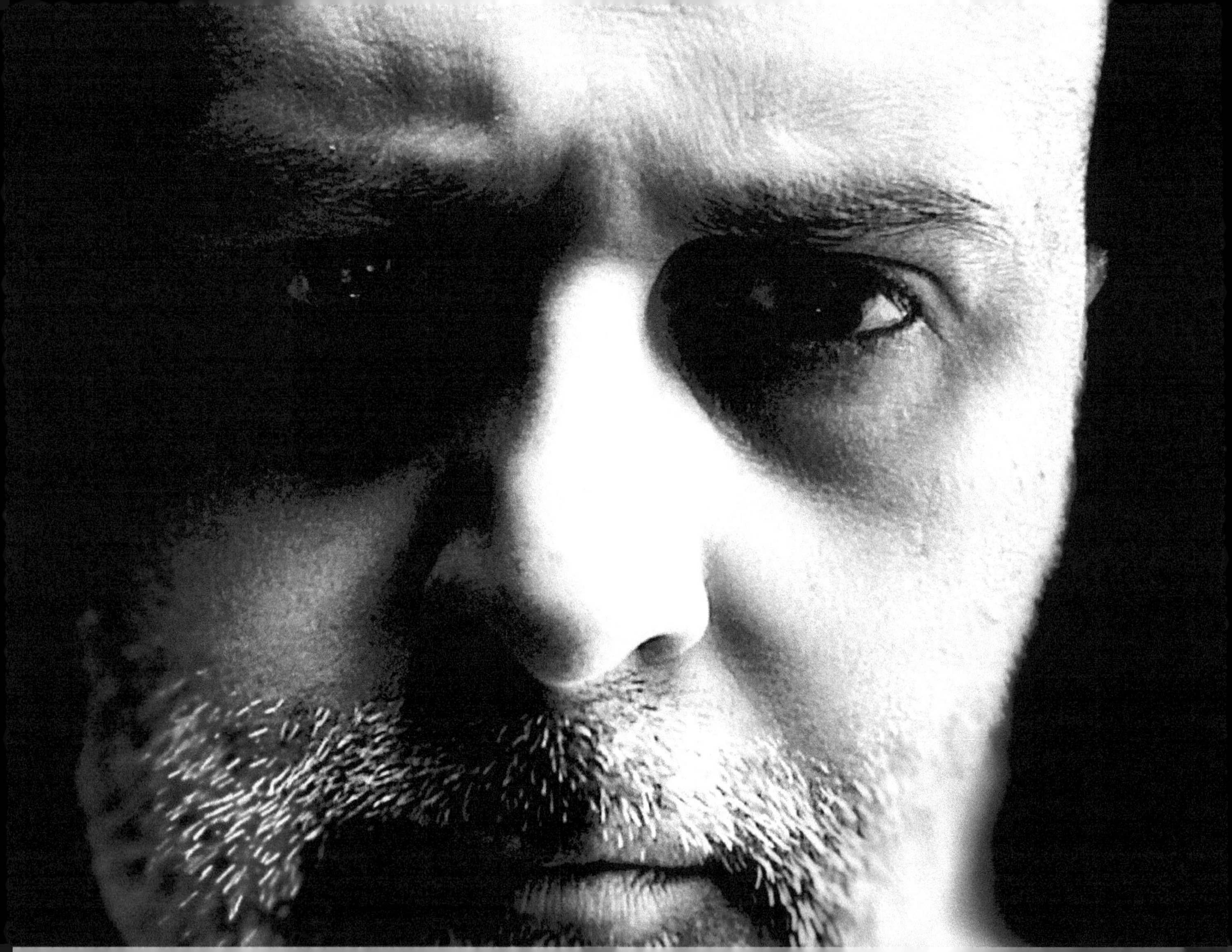

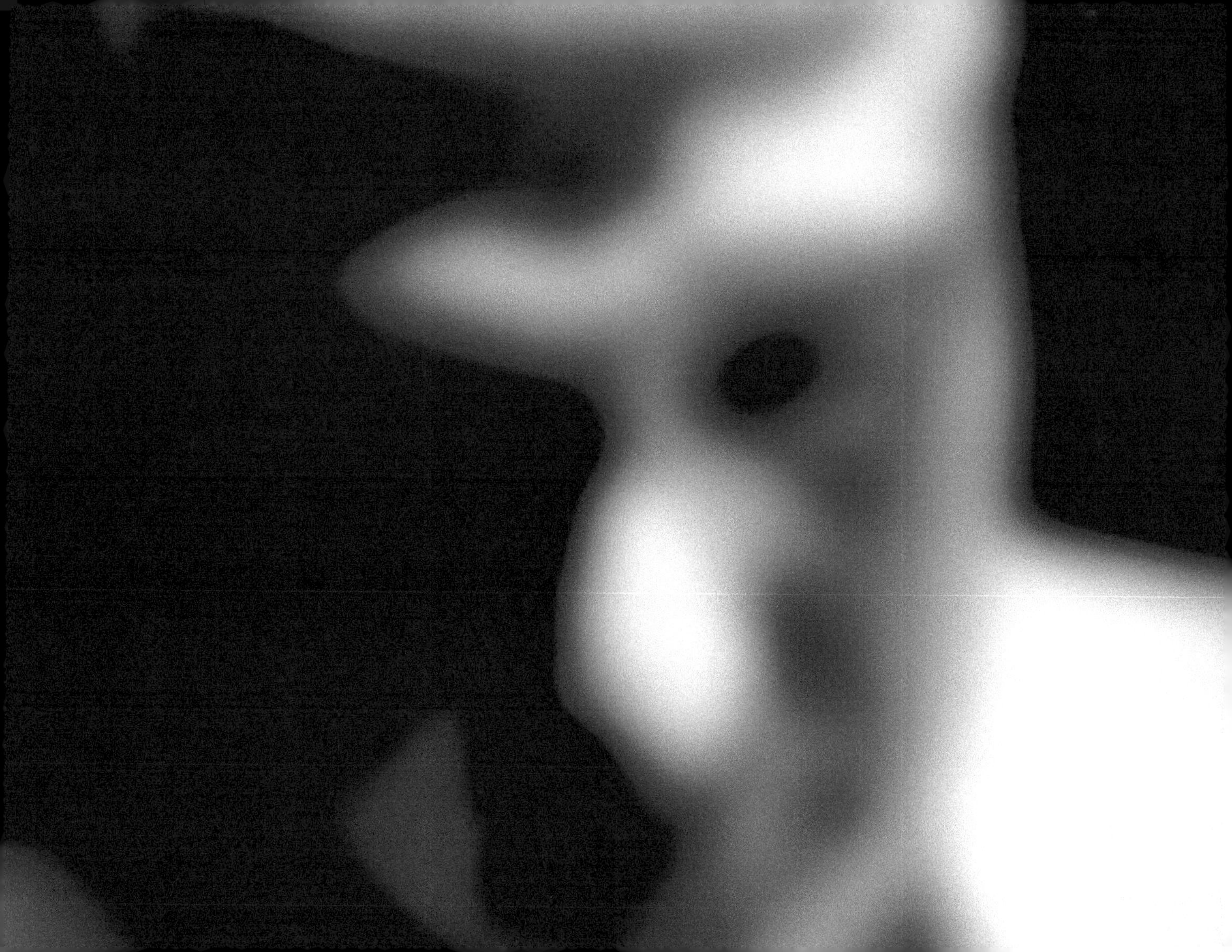

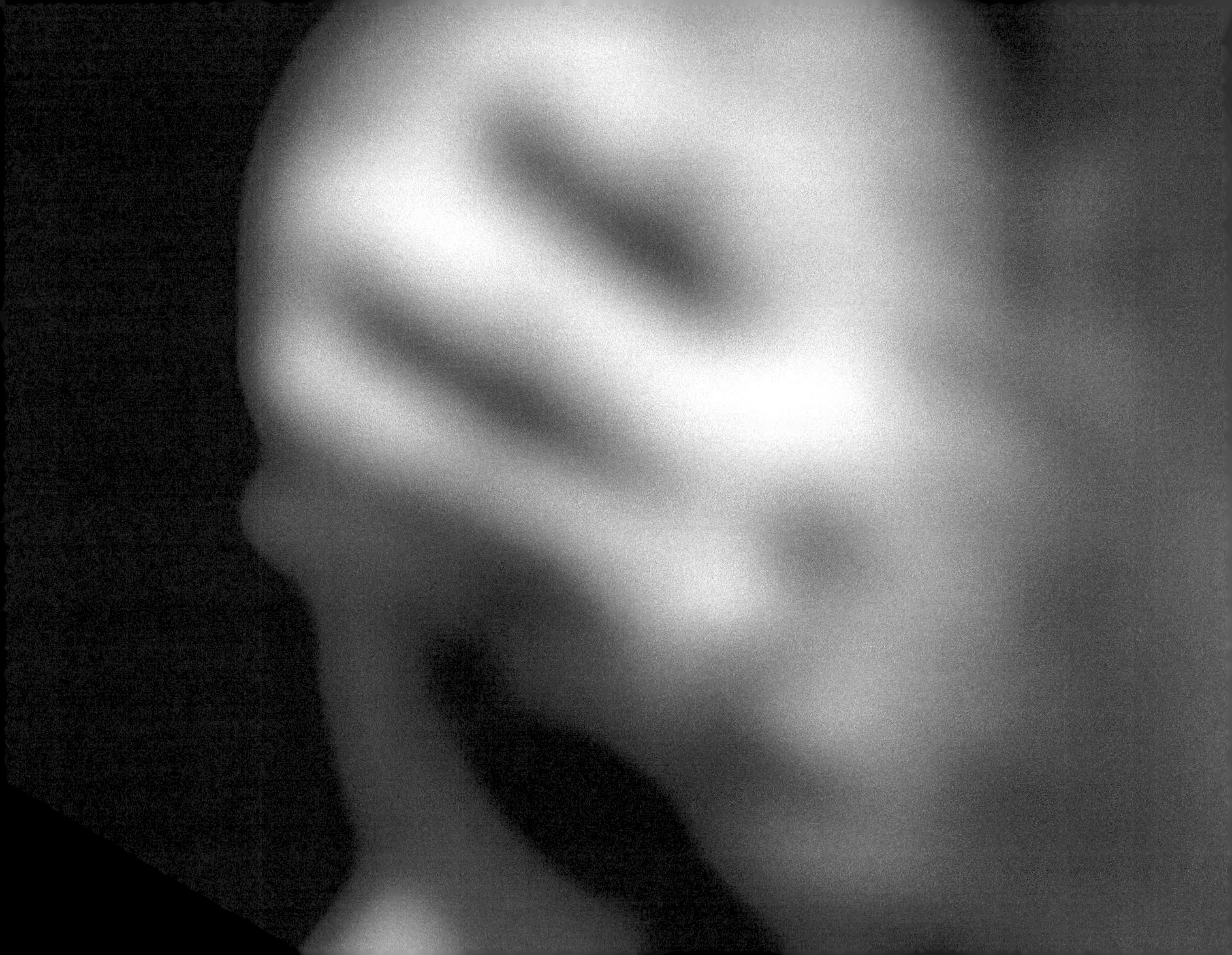

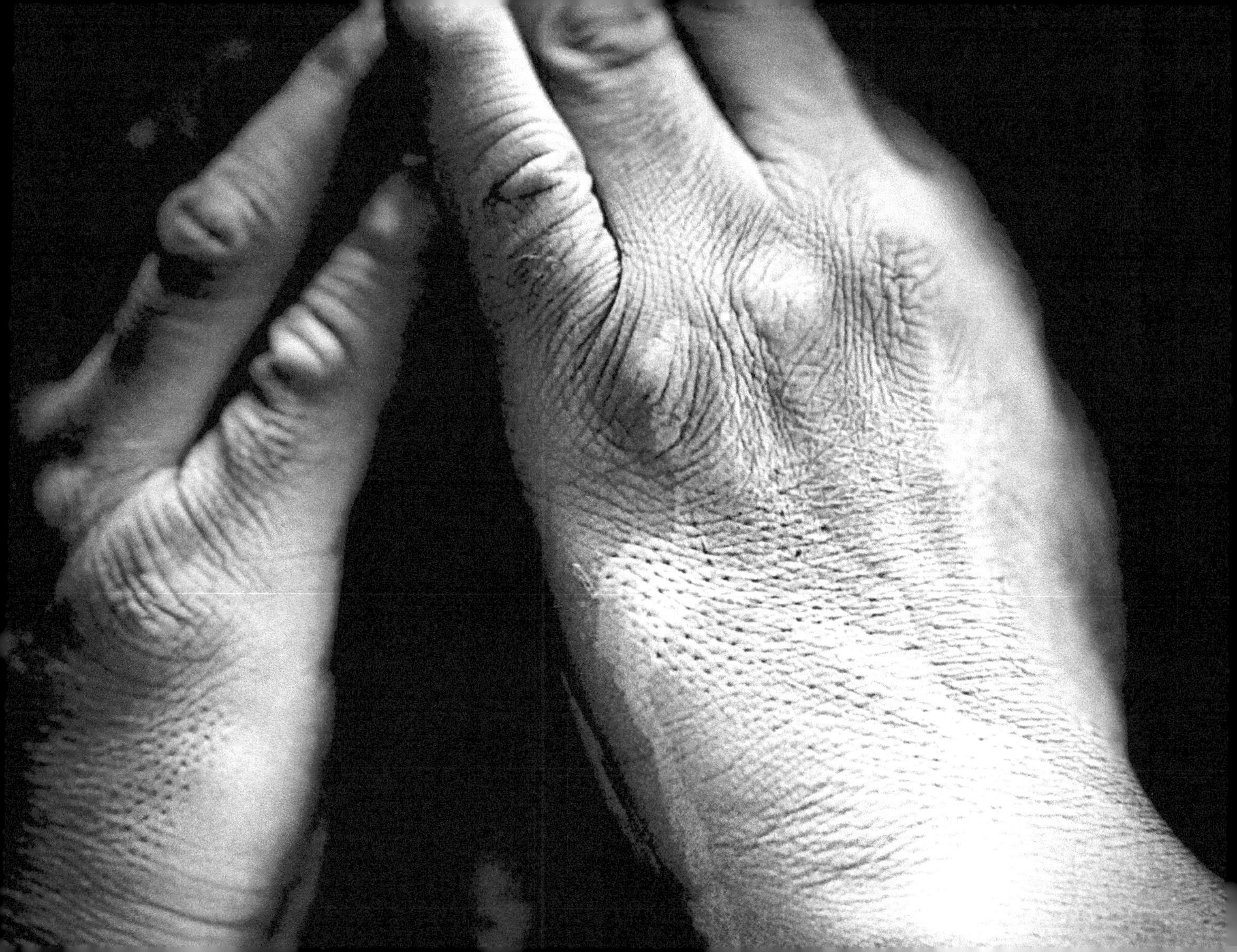

Silence stifles me

Deafening

As thoughts scream to be heard

Noises to be made

Desperation clenches it's sickening hold

On dreams that wish to be

But never can

Only fury remains

Where passion is lost

Sadness surrounds

Wrapping my waist

Like a desperate lover

Wanting me

Taking me

Taunting me

Memories of a familiar past

Teasing me

As tears fall silently to the ground

Remembrance of those I once knew

Of a father I once had

Of a joy I once felt

Emptiness fills me

Its breath thick

Seeking my center

My essence

Its heaviness passes thorough

Where is the love that revives?

One that fulfills?

Her presence is longed for

Desired

Needed

A scream builds within

Ready to call her

So that she may know my heart

My yearning

My dreams

Songs play on the radio

Harmonies of love lost

Fill me with sadness

Sorrow comes so easy

Where is the joy?

Won't the pain leave?

It's not my turn now

Let it find some other soul

To torture

With its wicked hold

Take it from me

I don't want it

Take it from me

I don't need it

This thing which you gave

Now only consumes

Where pleasure once thrived

Only pain now survives

Take this damn thing

As it eats me alive

Freedom is emptiness

Loneliness

Sadness

Nobody shares my bed

My thoughts

No smile adorns my lips

Agony must be dealt with

Laughter is stifled

Only I can hear

Myself

Alone

Lying alone

Here in my free prison

Emptiness fills the void

Anger resides

No thoughts

Only confusion

Twisted emotions

Stab the heart

Walls to be filled

Canvas to be painted

Never to be done

Nothing to be achieved

Never born

Is the dream

Shhhhhh

Listen to the quiet

Cacophony of sound

Deafening torment

My bed

My bed is my island

My sanctuary

My solace and refuge

My shame and remorse

Here I lie with lost dreams and dead goals

I push away the pain from under heavy sheets

Pain of family

Of abuse

Of neglect

I bury my head deep into my pillow and wish it away

No more tears nor memories

Only darkness and lost thoughts

You can't hurt me on this island

You can't cross this soft ocean

Your reach stops at the shores of the door

Your bitter physical sting is here no more

Scars of the soul fade into the darkness of the room

As the day turns to night

The night to dreams

The dreams to nightmares

Nightmares to screams

The heart goes blank

The dawn absorbs all

My bed is my sanctuary

My Island

Hard to love

Wanting to feel

Hurting to hold

Hollow in my heart

Pain in my veins

I know

I feel

I need

I want

But

Am I deserving?

You hurt me
But I hurt me more
The pain you caused was great
But the pain I create is deeper
You destroyed my flesh
But I destroy my soul
The scars you carved have healed
But the scars I carve are raw
You stunted my emotions
But I have blackened their growth
You made the monsters real
But I fed them

Anxiety has a sickening hold
Clenching my chest
Squeezing my heart
Piercing my lungs
Pounding my head
Driving deep
Into my brain
Through my skull
Scream now
Scream louder
SCREAM

Anger swells inside

Rage

Confusion

Darkness

Sadness

Torture

So much ache

Too much anguish

Memories of childhood

Haunt the adult

I am human, I say

Are you not?

I remember

The sweet ripe smell of my father's guilt

Whether your palm, belt or fist

Your hurt filled the air with mangoes

Plump delicious mangoes

Like the fat welts on our skin

Your admission of pain

Provoked the purchase of fruit

The deeper the cry

The greater your guilt

The juicier our reward

Virus ails the body
Loneliness infects the soul
Bodies heal
While hearts die
The shell that is present
Hides the torment within
One controls the other
But which one shall win?

Obscene is the dream

As I wake in the night

A sickness in the head

Brings a gleam as I cry

Pain comes not

From the lash

On the skin

But

From the jab

At the soul

Music plays

Songs from so long ago

Cast distant thoughts

From when blood would flow

Of childhood misery

Of innocence betrayed

No turning it off

Neither the music

Nor the blows

So much suffering

So powerful

I know

All this remains

Nothing lets go

I loved you

You loved me

We loved each other

We loved together

I used you

You used me

We used each other

We used together

I hurt you

You hurt me

We hurt each other

We hurt together

Pleasure.

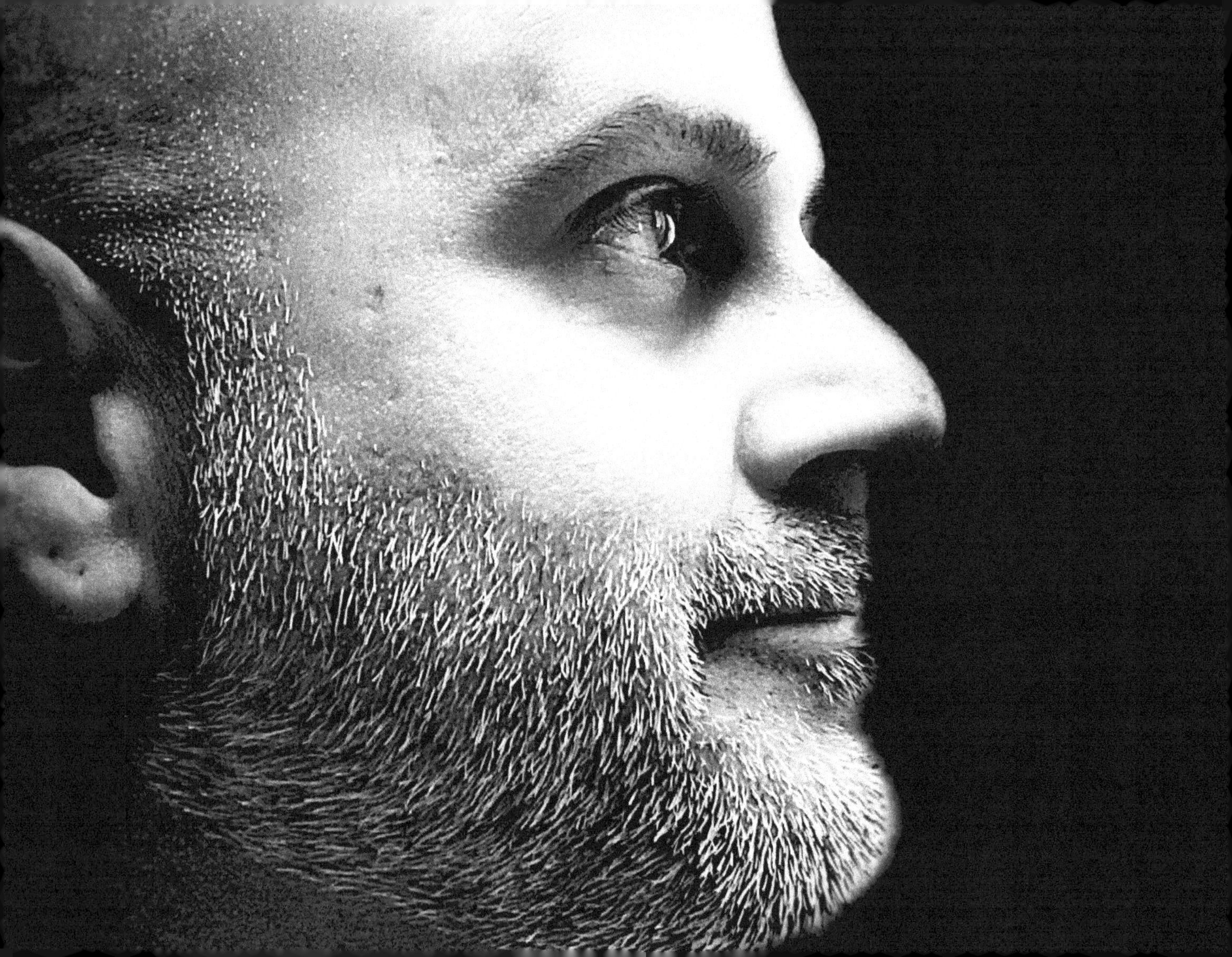

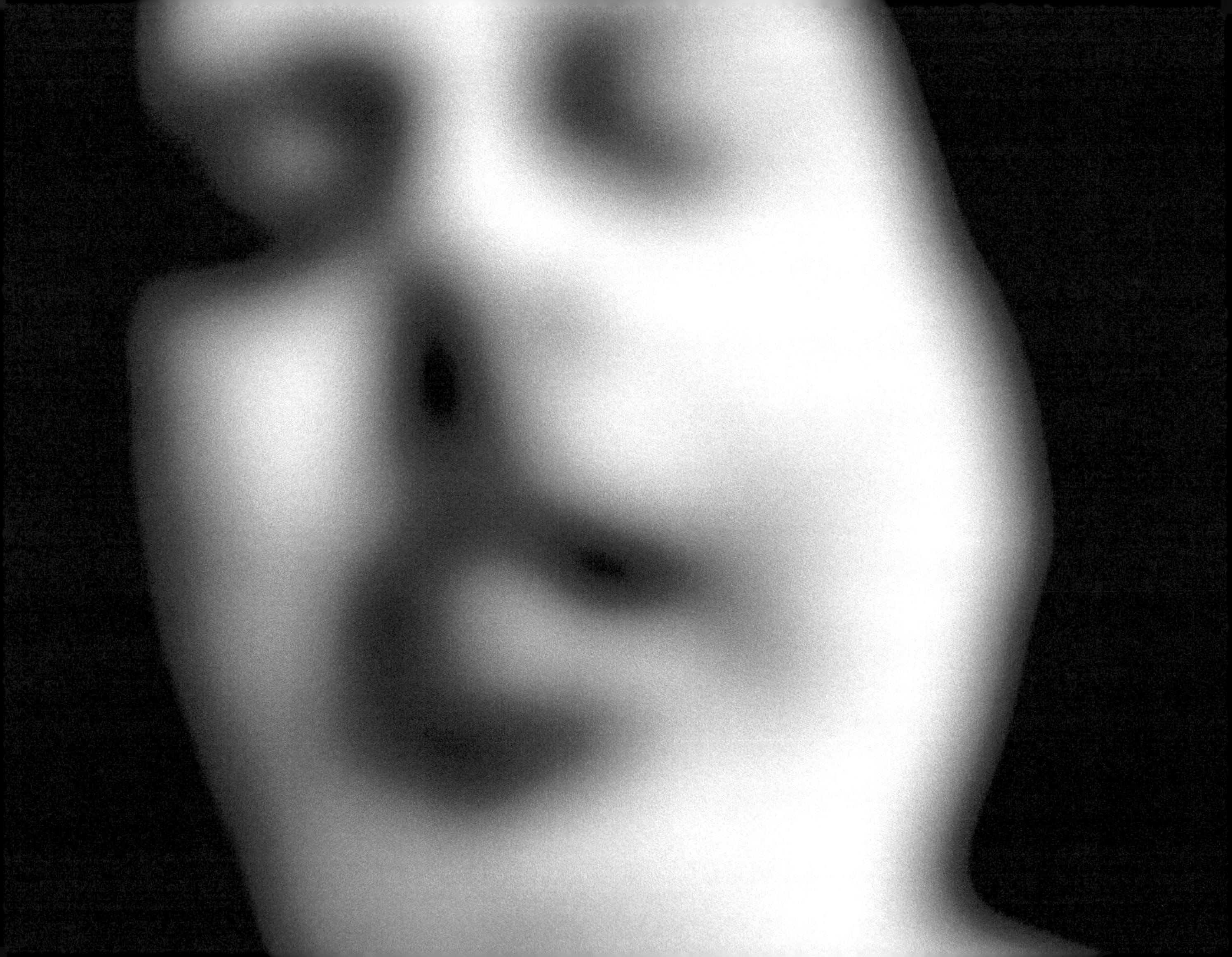

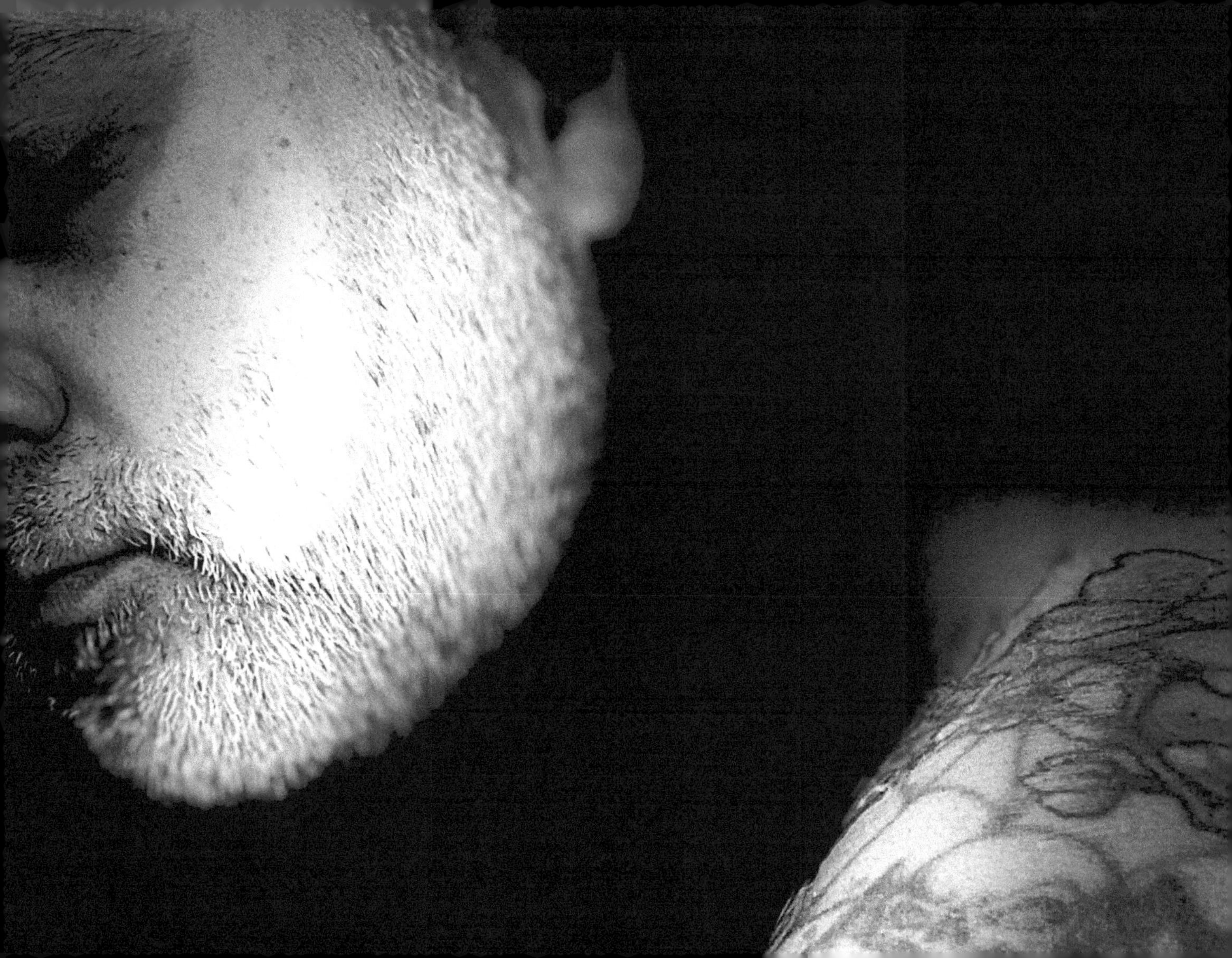

Wintry cold steel
Wraps my wrists
Biting
Bleeding
Exciting
Soothing

Sweet sting

Indulges pleasure

Her flesh absorbs

Devouring all

Pulling

Tempting

Promising

Pricks my back

Breathe yearning for release

Struggle to see

But forced not to

Bodies knowing

Only commands

Passion

Skin

Sweat

Taste

Pleasure

As sleep leaves
I reach for her
Letting fingers glide
Over warm tender skin
Feeling such softness
Gently she stirs under touch
Playing in dreams
Which fill her head
An angelic smile rests upon her lips
Bringing a warmth
Which I carry with me always

She fills my mind
All things stop
An emotional blur
No thoughts
Only feelings
Emptiness
Joy
Fulfillment
Inspiration
Pain
Ecstasy
I need to touch her
See her
Smell her
Fill myself with such warm sweet addiction
Feel her through my skin
Hear her in my sleep

Passion floods
Flows through my veins
Swims in my heart
Screams to be heard
Felt
Touched
Longs for escape
Seeps from me
Breaks its constraints
Seeks her
Guiding me
Making me let go
So that it may once again
Feel

I touch her
Thoughts are clear
Yet none matter
She touches me
Sensations
Fill me
Pour
Through me
Skin on skin
Thrills
Satisfies
Pacifies
We melt together
Nothing else matters

With you

Nights are brighter

Thoughts are clearer

I feel complete

I am complete

You hear me

Encourage me

Love me

I know you

Are the one

There is no other

I know this love

So true, so strong

Come back to me

I will wait for you

My heart will wait for you

Through blurry eyes

I see her

Light surrounds her

Clearing fuzziness within my head

Calmness calls me

As her brightness

Fills me

With all that she is

Tender is her touch
A furious passion
Just beneath the surface
She comes to me
Lays with me
Shares with me
Caresses me
All fears fade
Time disappears
Our flesh is one
Our thoughts few
Her pleasure
My joy

Sweetness emanates from her skin

Lingering on fingertips

I touch her

She flows into me

Filling my blood

With excitement

A wanting desire

To feel her soft warm skin

Next to mine

To hold her through the night

Once more

The heart bursts

A thousand explosions

Eyes embrace visions of color

The man resides

In warmth of memories

A smile as she sleeps

A sweet laugh from her lips

Her hand in his

Her sweet taste

Lingers

On my tongue

Fills my head

Swarms my mind

Eyes closed

I feel her tenderness

Just beneath me

Nipples harden

Touch

A whisper sends her

A caress brings heat

Her mouth brings ecstasy

Her secret is revealed

As mine is absorbed

Sweet earthy grass

Under

Big bulging clouds

Bright blue sky

A dogs smell of sunshine

As he lies in the warmth

My lovers smile

As she plays in dreams

The shine of a million stars

On a clear black night

All make life good

Important

Remarkable

Always

Radiant eyes

Beautiful shine

Secret smile

Only I can know

Heart so full

I can no longer control

Beauty unlike another

Within

Without

Most true thing

I will ever know

Black core

Suffocates self

Shiny shell wraps and binds

Smothers thoughts

Embraces dark

She brings light

She is light

Extinguishes doubt

She brings life

Hope

Joy

Love

She is love

Love is thick

Love is dense

Love is rich

It smells luxurious

It tastes divine

Her love always soothes
While her touch makes me move
Her beauty excites
Invites
My desire for her
She is everything
Everything I need
Everything I bleed
Her love is my light
My guide
My sun
She radiates passion
Inspires joy
She is everything
Everything I need
Everything I bleed

You love me

As only you can

You heal me

As only you can

You encourage me

As only you can

You warm me

As only you can

You hold me

As only you can

You wipe my tears

As only you can

Only you

Only you

Only you can

Once inside

Her world

Is mine

Perspective.

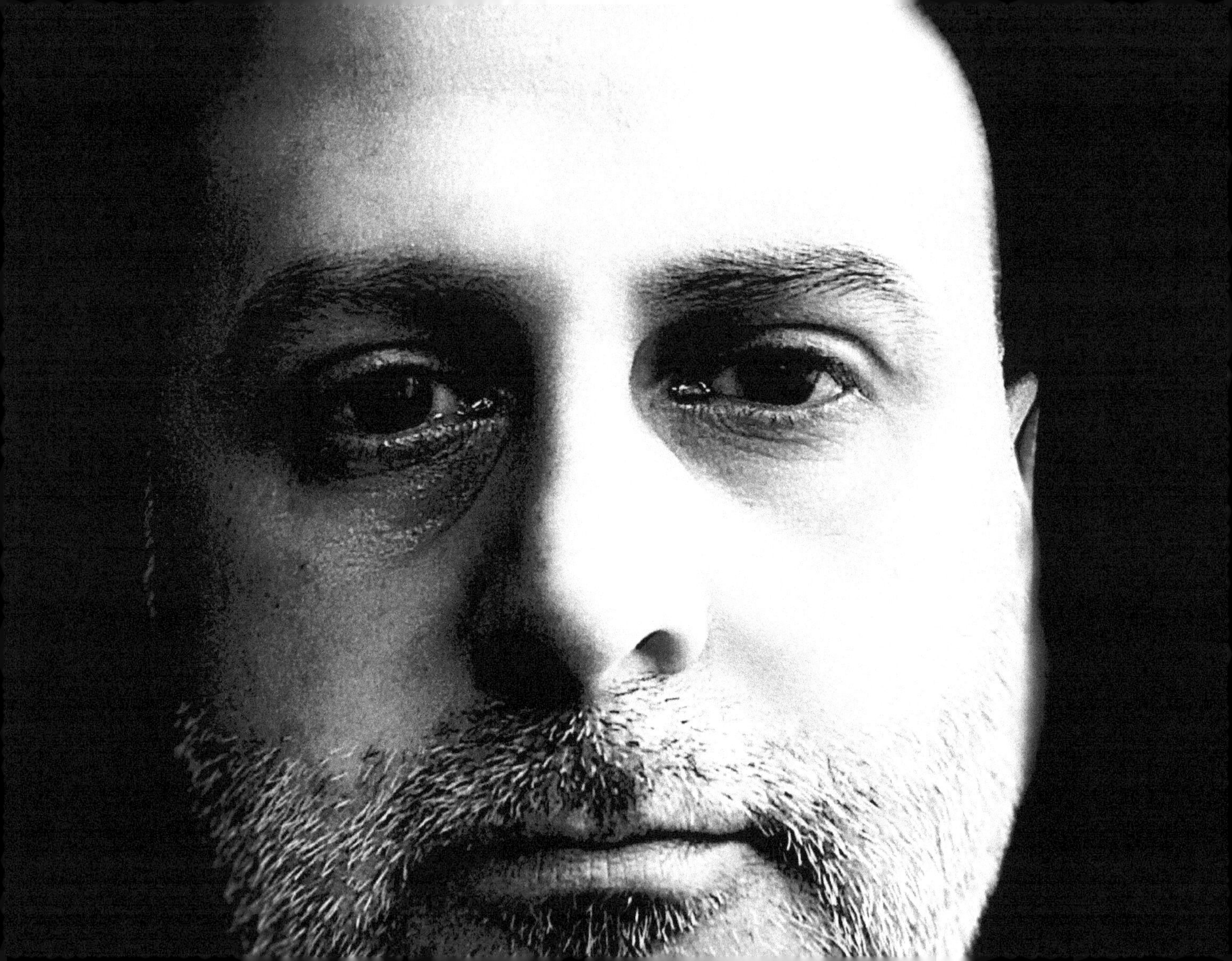

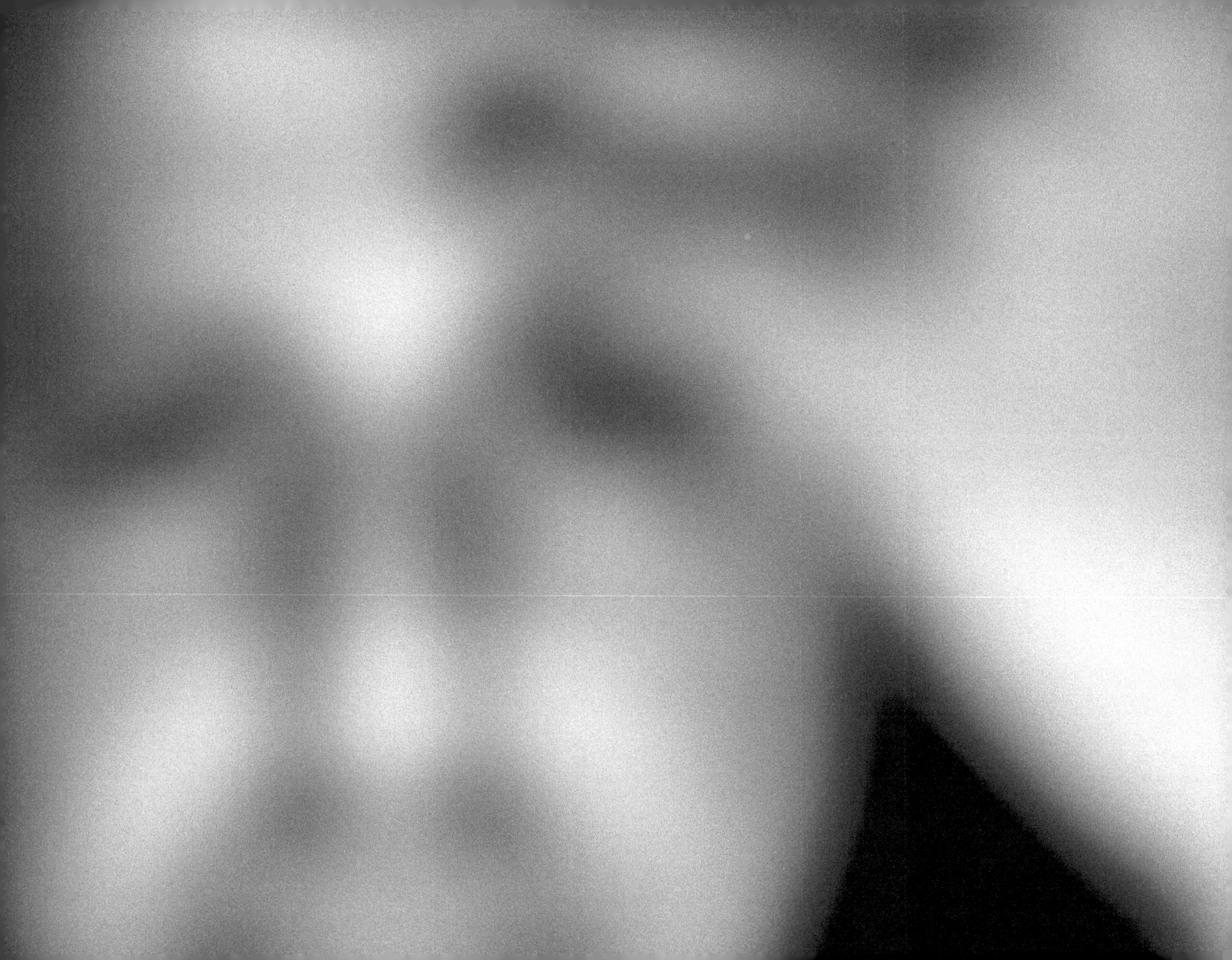

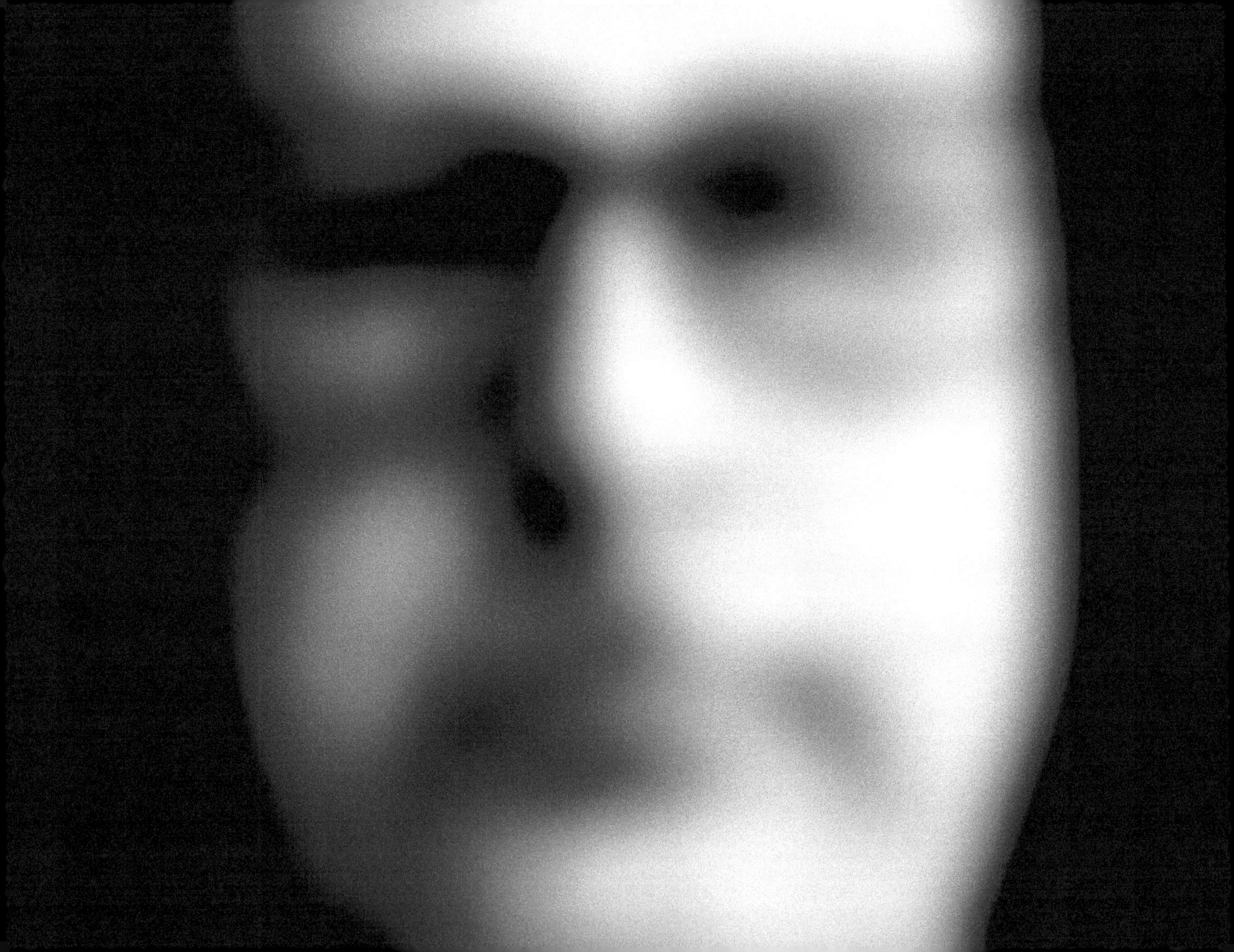

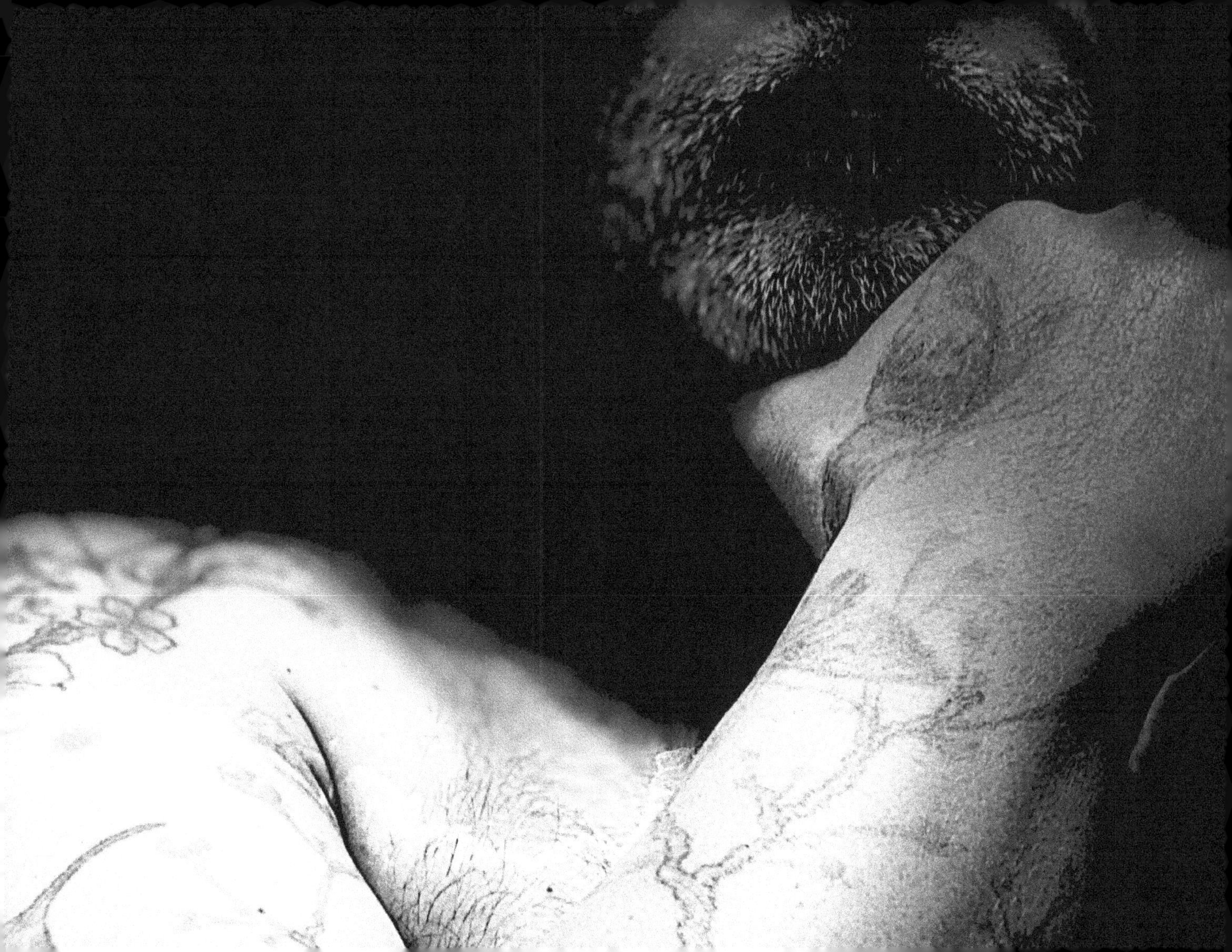

Frustrations fill me

Draining

Pulling

Playing with my mind

Whipping my soul

Do I have the strength to be

That which I desire?

Will I be only what I see?

Or more than my father was?

Can you hear me?

Do you watch me?

Guide me?

Do your thoughts flow through me?

Help me?

Teach me?

My heart is still full

Oh so many things

Which should have been said

But only were thought

I miss you

Knowing

I can never share

Stories

Joys

Emotions

Are you there?

Do you see me?

I hope you know

Why do I play the fool?
That's not the role I desire
I smile and laugh for all
Except myself
When I'm alone
Everything changes
The pain that lies
Beneath the surface
Comes out
And rears its filthy face
Life is a big act
Everyone plays a part
Some fools better than others

They say They believe in God

They believe in Money

They don't believe in Us

Yet We believe in Them

They show Us what to believe

Who to believe

How to believe

What We should be

They are all that We aspire

Yearn for

Pray to

Seek to become

Follow Their dreams

Abandon Your own

If You believe that

You're already gone

I am invisible

Invincible

Powerful

Powerless

Well versed

Deaf mute

All of the above

None of the above

Who knows me?

I can't know myself

Be empty

That's easiest

Disappear

Not fitting

Wanting to know

Needing to know

Who can show me?

Guide me?

Take me where I belong

Ghosts surround me

Their presence felt

Their sight unseen

Their memories linger

Their thoughts remain

I remember

Wanting more than their spirit can offer

Needing more

Getting nothing

It moves

Touching

Seeing

Tasting

Sensing

Life flows through it

Death passes from it

Screams

Shouts

Silence

Nothing

Sit down

Stand up

Speak

Think

Shut up

Piss

Fuck

Abstain

Do as I say

Do as I do

Paint the white fence

Raise the kids

Go to work

Create more debt

Pay the mortgage

Live their life

Not your own

Heart strains

Lungs stress

Mind races

Sweat

Fear

Stop

Breath

In

Out

Control this life

Or

This life controls you

Pain

Pleasure

Perspective

Life Edited

Love yourself

Love yourself

Love yourself

Don't

Love yourself

Love yourself

Love yourself

Can't

Love yourself

Love yourself

Love yourself

Won't

Love yourself

Love yourself

Love yourself

Never

Love yourself

Love yourself

Love yourself

Home is my heart

Home is my comfort

Home is my shelter

Home is my castle

Home is my fortress

Home is my prison

On a downtown bus
Life passed me by
It didn't bother stopping
It just waved goodbye
Where you going?
Was my only cry
To the end of the line
Where you'll die
You'll die

Star light, star bright

Oh brother, where art thou tonight?

In the hills?

Amongst the streets?

Do shoes remain on your feet?

Does your hunger grow?

Is your thirst complete?

Will your mind finally shatter?

Will your illness retreat?

Oh how I wish more

For your life to be sweet

A return to no burdens

Where you may find peace

America has a virus

Pandemic so complete

Hate

Anger

Blame

Contaminate the air

Sucked in

Heaved out

Through filthy infected lungs

Her cure

Empathy

Compassion

Truth

All discarded

Dumped

Disposable

Like used condoms

Stopping the love

From penetrating deep inside

I will not think bad thoughts

I will not think bad thoughts

I will not think bad thoughts

I will not think bad thoughts

I will not think bad thoughts

I will not think bad thoughts

I will not think bad thoughts

I will not think bad thoughts

I will not think bad thoughts

I will not think

Bad thoughts

I will not think

I will not

Think

Fuck them
Their fascist uniforms
Their Nazi salutes
Boys become men
Men become monsters
Filled with doubt
And desire
Sadistic intents
Inspire indifference
At campfires
No understanding
Of others
You isolate those
That would bring respite and reprieve
And hurt a boy that only wanted to be

Look in the mirror

Make it crack

Fuck that person

Looking back

I embrace the dark

Night

Black

Shadow

Gloom

Depth

Despair

Because

There is light on the other side

Being alone
My mind wanders
Part of everything
Part of nothing
Indulge myself
Deprive myself
I have clarity
I lose focus
I realize
I know something
Yet know nothing

Your actions

May never

Save your soul

But they

Sometimes

Save your

Skin

Are you defined

By

Your clothes

Your watch

Your shoes

Your car

Your house

Your education

Your wealth

Your ignorance

Your indifference

Your inaction?

about

Jameel Haiat grew up in Los Angeles as the son of two cultures.
Born to a Pakistani father and a Mexican/American mother, he
is a product of their angst, turmoil, love and attention.
His writings reflect the trauma of childhood loss and pain, love
lost and gained and reflections upon his place in the world from
a multi-cultural upbringing.

His life as a successful artist, writer, maker and designer has
taken him to places far and abroad where he has absorbed
other cultures, personal stories and perspectives that influence
his work today.

He now lives in Chiang Mai, Thailand with his loving wife and
partner in everything, Hilcia and their beautiful doggie daughter
Tomi Yum.

book

Life Edited. Pain. Pleasure. Perspective. is a contemporary
collection of poetry and spoken word in remembrance of
childhood loss and pain, love lost and gained, perspectives and
musings of our world today.
It's a look in the mirror and a reflection upon what hurts, heals
and makes us human…